GOYA

BETWEEN TWO WORLDS

Edward Lucie-Smith

Cv/Visual Arts Research Series208

Goya
Between Two Worlds

Edward Lucie-Smith

ISBN: 9781910110270

Cv Publications www.tracksdirectory.ision.co.uk

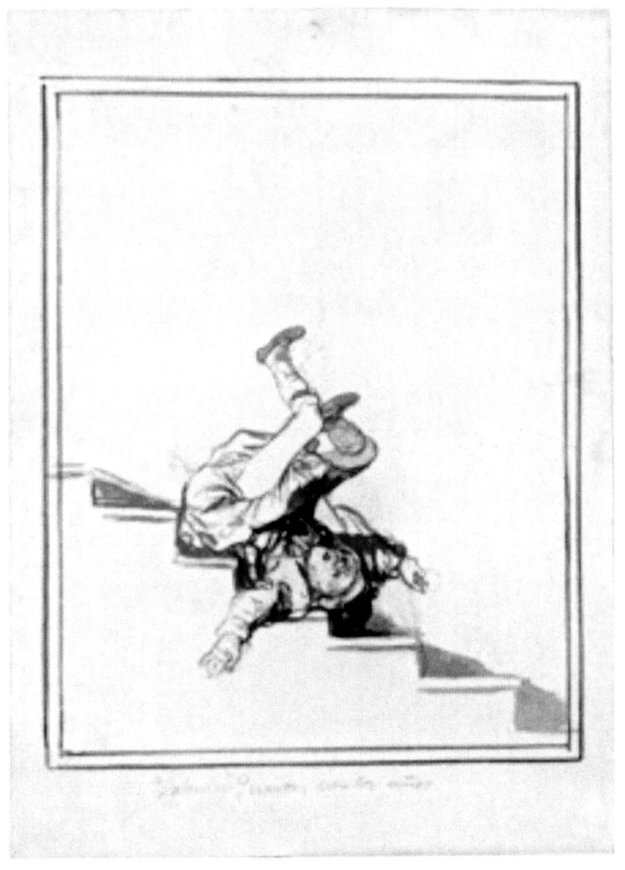

Francisco Goya, (1746-1828)
Valentias? Quenta con los anos (Showing off? Remember your age)
'Black Border' Album (E), page 7 c. 1816-20Brush and black ink with wash and scraping 266 x 186 mm Berlin, Staatliche Museen zu Berlin Preussischer, Kulturbesitz, Kupferstichkabinett, kdz 4395

GOYA BETWEEN TWO WORLDS

'Goya – the Witches and Old Women Album', now on view at the Courtauld Gallery in London, is fascinating for many reasons. It is a brilliant example of painstaking detective work. The long separated drawings of this album, which dates from 1819-23, have been brought together in their original sequence. Only one sheet, out of 23, now appears to be missing. It also represents a bridge between once traditional ideas about art and those we have now. Some of its roots are in the long-established tradition of personal caricature, and the related tradition of grotesque genre portraits of the poor and disadvantaged. Remote, but still present, are echoes of the little grotesque figures made in Hellenistic Alexandria. One can also see traces of influence from 17th century and later caricature drawings – those made, for example, by Guercino and Pier Francesco Mola.. Even more strongly visible are what Goya owed to the drawings made by Giandomenico Tiepolo – the Punchinello series in particular. Giandomenico lived and worked in Spain from 1762-70, as assistant to his father, G.B. Tiepolo.

What is highly original is the fact that these drawings, often extremely ambiguous in meaning, form a meditative sequence, not apparently intended for public consumption, but entirely self-reflexive. They record the artist's dreams and fantasies, but strictly for his own contemplation. As such they represent a major psychological breakthrough, a next step forward from the late self-portraits of Rembrandt. Their successors are the images created by major Surrealist artists such as Salvador Dalì and Max Ernst. The exhibition enables us to see our contemporary ideas about the nature of the self at the very moment of their first formation.

Though the exhibition title invites the visitor to focus on the idea of witches – casters of spells, facilitators of the uncanny – it soon becomes apparent, when one looks at the drawings more closely, that the real subject is old age. At the time when the album was made, if the dating now offered is correct, Goya would have been in his seventies. That is to say, he and old age were personally acquainted. The artist did not die until he was 82 – he had an unusually long life span for a man of his time. He had survived the Napoleonic Wars, perhaps especially horrible in his country. He had also survived changing political regimes. He kept his position at the Spanish court after the Bourbon restoration, despite having worked for Joseph Bonaparte. The restored Ferdinand VII reportedly said to him: "You deserve to be garrotted, but you are a great artist so we forgive you." Goya expressed his contempt and dissatisfaction for the state of things in Spain in his last series of prints Los Disparates (The Follies), which were made during the same period as the series of drawings featured at the Courtauld. The prints were so sharply critical of the Spanish church and state that they could not be published in Goya's lifetime. They were first published in 1864, more than thirty years after the artist's death. Goya was in fact under so much pressure from the Spanish authorities in these final years that he left Spain in 1824, and moved to Bordeaux.

Los Disparates prompt comparisons not just with the Italian caricaturists already mentioned but also with work being done in Britain at he same time, and in particular with the images produced by James Gillray. One characteristic of caricature drawings, more or less throughout their history, and particularly if they contain any kind of allegorical element, rather than being just satirical portraits of particular individuals, is that they anticipate what later came to be called surrealism. The drawings shown at the Courtauld are often surrealist avant la lettre. The third drawing in the reconstructed series, for example, shows an old crone levitating as she strums on a guitar. She wears a frilly, embroidered dress, and has flowers in her hair, like some flirtatious gypsy entertainer, whom one would expect to be much younger. Beneath her sits another woman, apparently dressed as a nun. She is holding her nose, and seems to be looking up the guitar-player's skirts.

Another drawing, a little further along in the sequence, is entitled 'A Dream of Flogging'. It shows a group of four figures, once again floating in the air. Three are old women. The fourth is a half-naked man, whom one of the women is about to flog with a cowhide whip. The catalogue note for this drawing enters into some fairly elaborate explanations. First, it notes that the skimpy garment the male figure wears resembles a shroud. Next, it cites a Spanish tradition of flogging a corpse in order to bring it back to life through demonic possession. Next again it notes that the Spanish verb azotar – 'to whip' – often has sexual connotations, and that the motif of figures rising in the air if often a metaphor for the effects of sexual pleasure. Finally, it cites traditional carnival celebrations in Aragon and Catalonia where women were beaten, in an echo of old, pre-Christian fertility rites.

Old people and flying figures, are staple elements in this sequence of drawings. Flying or falling is sometimes presented as a metaphor for dreaming, as in the drawing with a single protagonist, probably male, which is entitled Pesadilla ('Nightmare'). This is one of the things that reinforces the idea that the drawings in this series can legitimately be regarded as proto-surrealist, fore-shadowings of thing that the 20th century Surrealist Movement was to bring to fruition.

Another over-riding characteristic of the drawings is, quite simply, that they were private – made by a man using this means to hold a conversation with himself. In this, they differ from the prints of the Disparates series. Though these, in the end, were never published during Goya's lifetime, the very fact that they are prints, not drawing – manufactured, multiple objects – argues that the artist must have envisaged a possible public for them. It also argues that other people, not just Goya himself, knew that a print series was being worked on. With the drawings, this was not necessarily the case.

If we think of the drawings as an intimate conversation – the self interrogating the self – there is perhaps one thing that we do well to remember is that Goya was profoundly deaf, as the result of an illness suffered in 1792-3. The house he occupied at the time when these drawings were made was called the Quinta del Sordo - the 'House of the Deaf Man' – so his deafness must by that time have been regarded as one of his defining characteristics. It was decorated with phantasmagoric paintings, the so-called Black Paintings, which certainly have some relationship to the drawings exhibited at the Courtauld. Executed in oil directly on the walls of the house, these paintings have been described by the Goya scholar Fred Licht as "the most essential to our understanding of the human condition in modern times, just as Michelangelo's ceiling is essential to understanding the tenor of the 16th century." This description is much too hyperbolic. Michelangelo's frescos in the Sistine were always intended for public scrutiny, if not, perhaps for the throngs of tourists who now come to the Vatican to see them. The Black Paintings are now visible in the Prado, in much damaged and over-painted condition, but they did not migrate there until as late as 1874, when they were taken down from their original position and rather brutally transferred to canvas. Before that they lurked in the private residence of someone who was become increasingly reclusive, not only because of his alienation from the restored Bourbon regime, but because of his disability.The paintings, as much as the drawings, belong to the private universe of a man deprived of one of his primary senses, more interested in his own meditations than in actually communicating to an audience, however small.

One of the things that tends to distinguish these drawings from 'normal' caricatures is that they are often ambiguous. There is no clear message. This ambiguity is so deep rooted in some of the images that one gets the feeling that they may sometimes have puzzled the artist himself. There is another drawing entitled Pessadilla or Nightmare, from very late in the sequence that scholars have now reconstructed. It shows an old hag carrying two skeletal male figures on her back. Originally it was called Vision, a title still legible but now crossed out. The exhibition catalogue claims that this change "demonstrates the importance [Goya] accorded to verbal as well as visual expression." I beg to differ. I think it illustrates the fact that the artist sometimes felt deeply uncertain about the significance of what his subconscious offered up to him.

The things the drawings openly say – their non-coded, non-hermetic messages – are disconcerting enough. While the exhibition curators would clearly like to put the emphasis on witches and witchcraft, seeing this link to the supernatural and uncanny as something that joins Goya, in his later years, to the Europe-wide Romantic Movement, what strikes me is their fascination, one might almost say their obsession, with the idea of old age. My approach to them comes from the fact that I am now even older than Goya was when he created these images. To a spectator of my years, he says; "Hey, look at this, bro – we're both in the same boat."

Goya's old people are quite often boisterous, often undignified. Two old women fight – the caption points out that Old Women Fight Too. On the next sheet in the sequence, an old woman stands solo, bent, heavily draped, leaning on a stick. She stares blankly into the distance. The caption comments: What folly, still to be thinking of marriage. Another drawing, of an equally decrepit old dame, shows her with a cat, The beast has its back to her, and is ready to pounce on something beyond the edge of the sheet. The caption says drily: She talks with her cat. In yet another drawing, Goya portrays a long-established Spanish literary archetype, the procuress La Celestina. She is seated at a table loaded with small bottles that may contain various potions, aphrodisiacs maybe, or perhaps something more noxious. In her right hand she dangles what is apparently a rosary, emblem of her sanctimonious mode of operation, outside convents and in churches.

The final drawing surviving from the album shows, not an old woman or old women, but an old man, bent over, hobbling along with the help of two sticks. The eloquent tag-line is: Just can't go on at the age of 98. The catalogue prudently compares to an even later drawing made when Goya had made his escape to Bordeaux, that is to say, very shortly before his death. It shows another old man, now with a long white beard, again hobbling on two sticks. The caption is considerably more hopeful. It says: I'm Still Learning. This doesn't altogether remove the impression made by the sequence of sheets exhibited at the Courtauld that Goya's view of the world, during the concluding years of his career, was a profoundly pessimistic one. Rembrandt's drawings of old men. Including those made in the closing years of career, give his subjects dignity. The same is true, maybe even more so, of his painted portraits of old men. Dignity is not a term one can easily associate with any of these drawings by Goya.

What Goya offers – offers himself, one must remember, not any outside audience – is a world regarded without illusions. He's not going to let himself off: this is the way it is. Despite the occasional sinister/romantic trappings – an example is the terrifying image called Dream of a Good Witch, which shows a decrepit hag hobbling along with a lot of babies hung from a pole, like so many live chickens ready for the pot – this surely isn't the kind of vision that the Romantic artists of the same epoch, but from elsewhere in Europe, shared. There's no real sturm und drang here. The storm has already blown itself out.

Goya was undoubtedly a great artist, but we shouldn't assume that great artists always have to provide us with positive messages. What one has in this album is a profoundly deaf man, living in a society he regards as catastrophic, musing privately about the human condition. If there is a positive note, it can be found in the sheer feistiness of the poor undignified elders he portrays. They are not going to let their situations get them down. They feel no impulse to be well-behaved or decorous. One can assume, I think, that Goya empathised with that. The message of the album, and the exhibition the Courtauld has built around it, is that "Things are as they are – like it or lump it." That's not a 'romantic' message, in any sense of the adjective, with a capital 'R' or without one. It might, however, be regarded as an apt message for our own times.

Edward Lucie-Smith
London March 2015

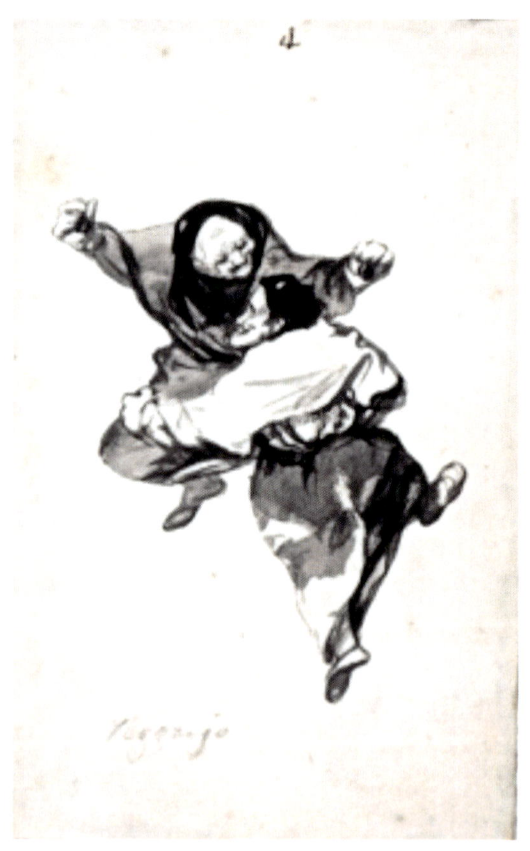

Francisco Goya (1746-1828)
Regozijo (Mirth) 'Witches and Old Women' Album (D), page 4
c. 1819-23Brush, black and grey ink with traces of red chalk and scraping
237 x 148mmNew York, The Hispanic Society of America

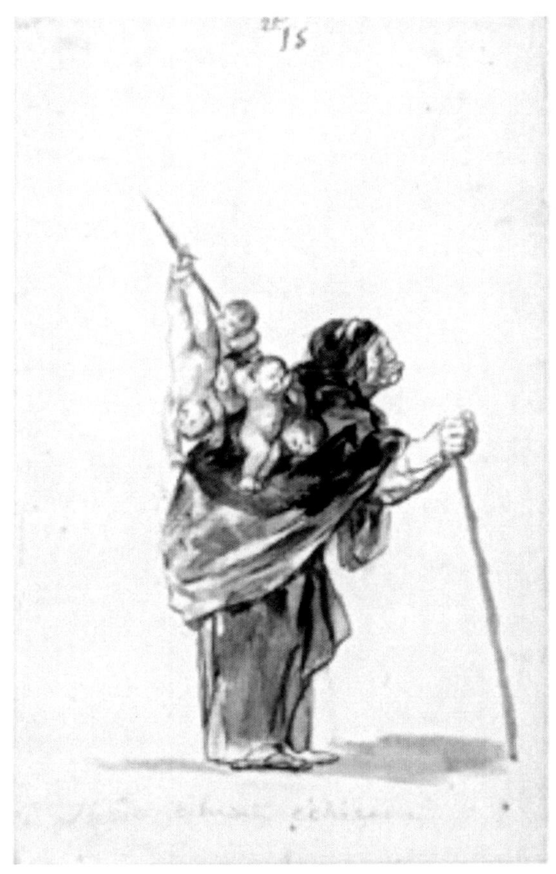

Dream of a good witch , c. 1819–23
Brush and black and grey ink 234 x 144 mm
Berlin, Staatliche Museen zu Berlin
Preussischer Kulturbesitz, Kupferstichkabinett

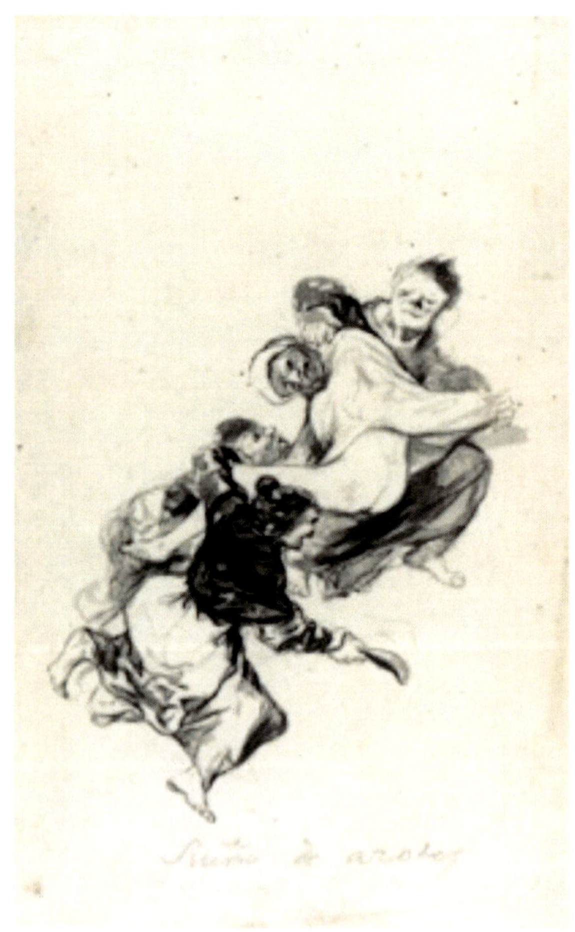

Francisco Goya (1746-1828)
Sueno de azotes (Dream of Flogging)
'Witches and Old Women Album' (D), page 6
c. 1819-23 Brush and black and grey ink over traces of graphite, 233 x 143 mm
Chicago, The Art Institute of Chicago, Clarence Buckingham Collection,

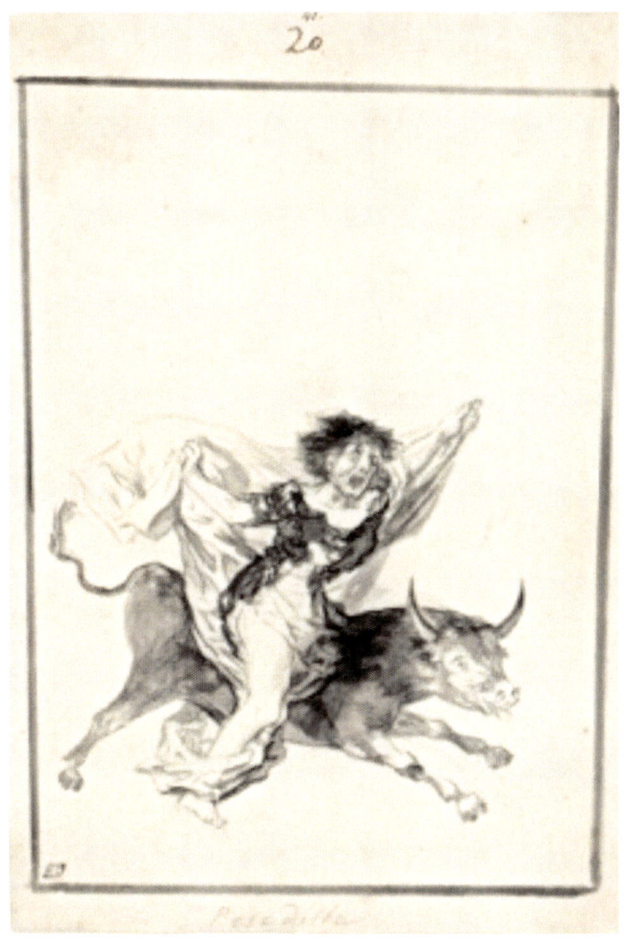

Francisco Goya (1746-1828)
Pesadilla (Nightmare)
'Black Border' Album (E), page 20
c. 1816-20Brush, black ink with wash and scraping
364 x 181 mm New York, The Morgan Library & Museum,

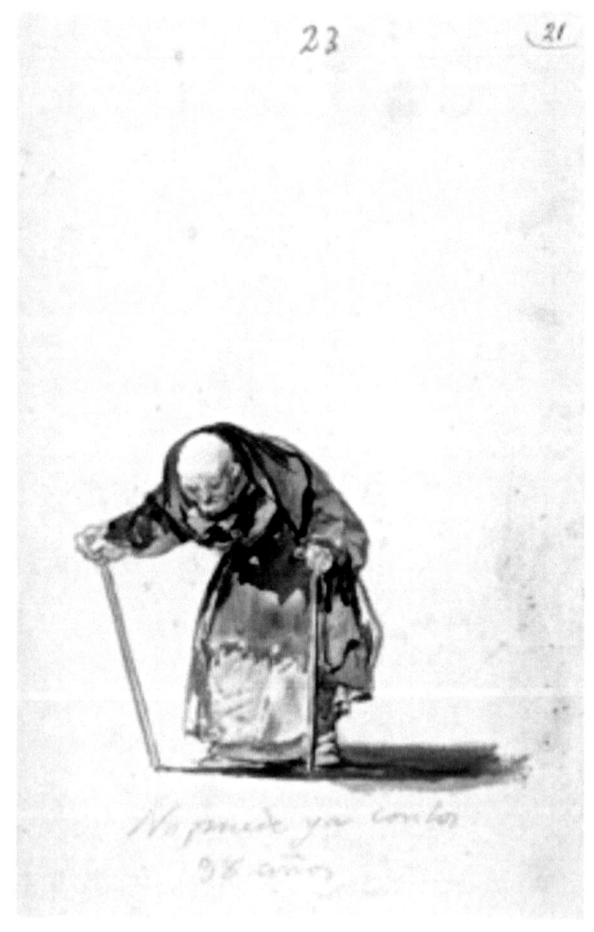

Francisco Goya (1746- 1828)
No puede ya con los 98 anos (Just can't go on at the age of 98)
'Witches and Old Women' Album (D), page 23
c. 1819-23 Brush, black and grey ink
233 x 144 mm Los Angeles, The J. Paul Getty Museum,

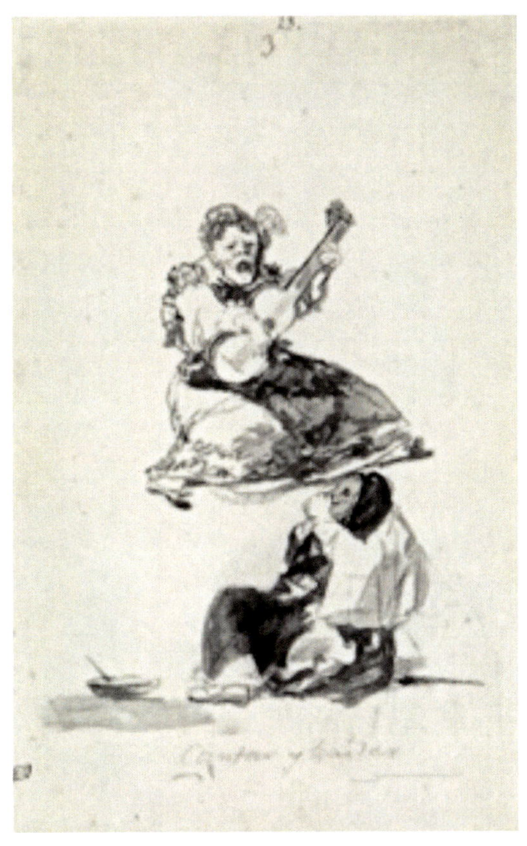

Francisco Goya (1746-1828)
Cantar y Bailar (Singing and dancing)
'Witches and Old Women Album' (D), page 3
c. 1819-23 Brush and black and grey ink with scraping
235 x 145 mm London, The Courtauld Gallery, Samuel Courtauld Trust,

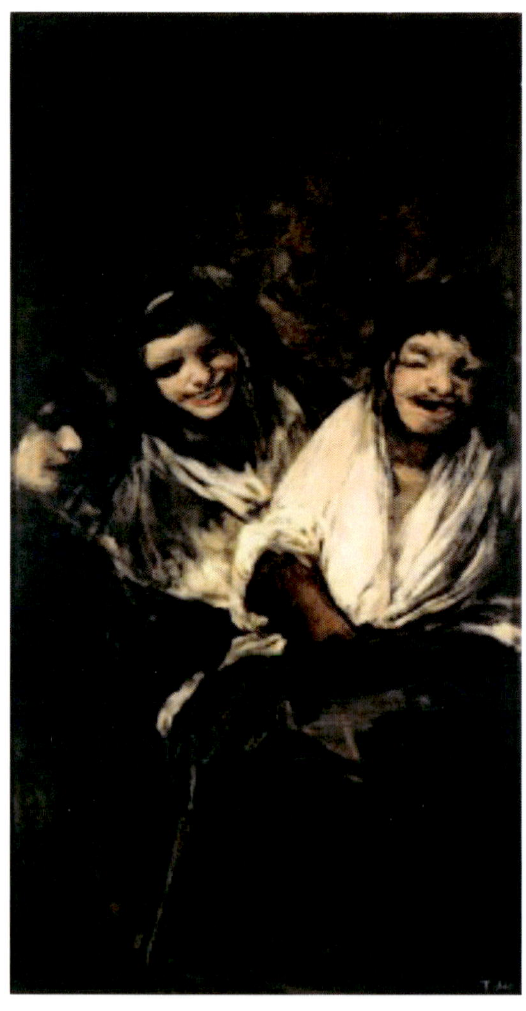

Women Laughing, 1819-1823

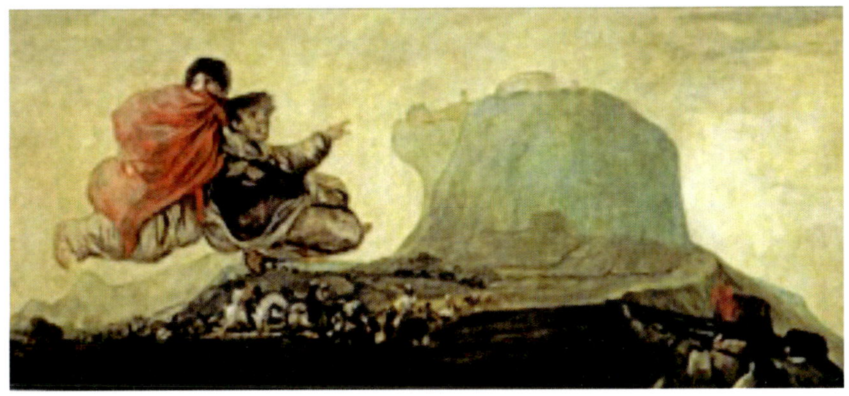

Fantastic Vision, 1819-1823

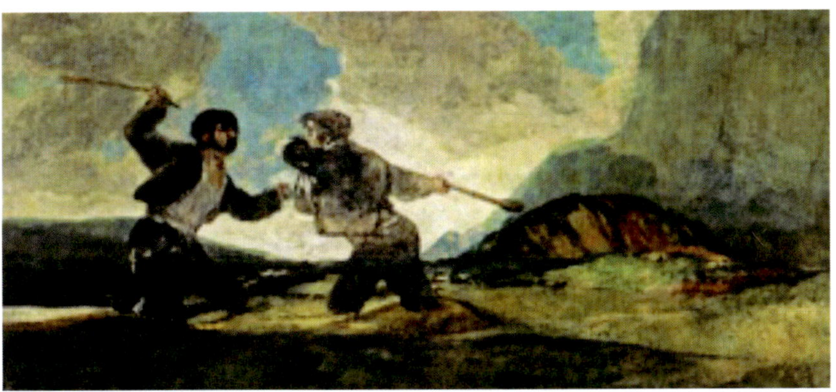

Fight with Cudgels,The Fates, 1819-1823

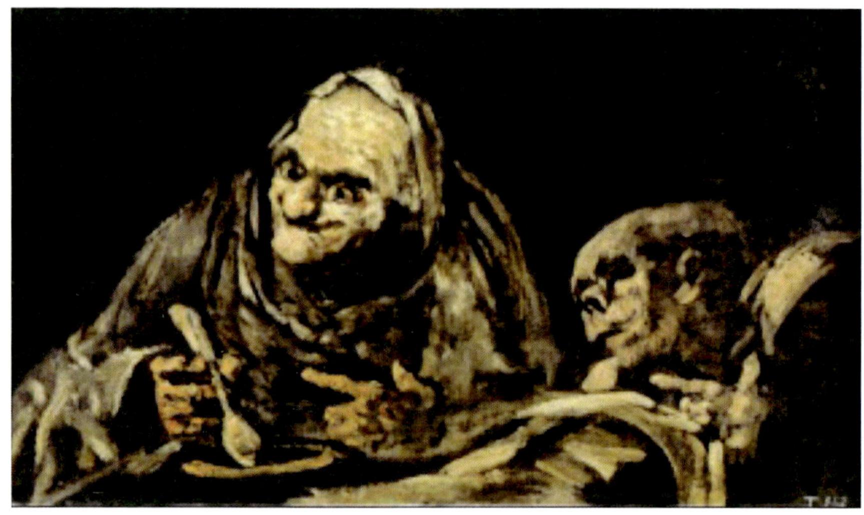

Two Old Men Eating Soup, 1819-1823

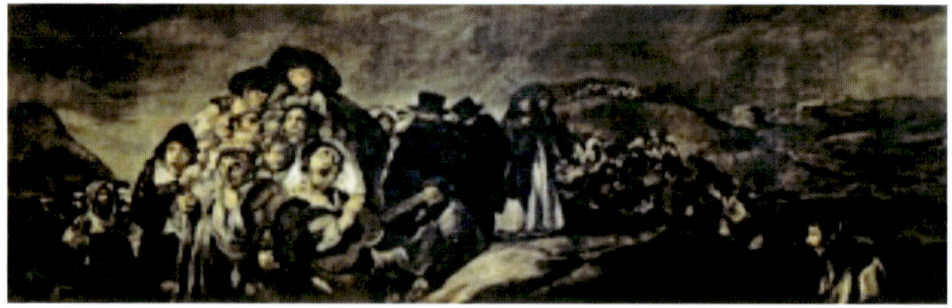

A Pilgrimage to San Isidro, 1819-1823

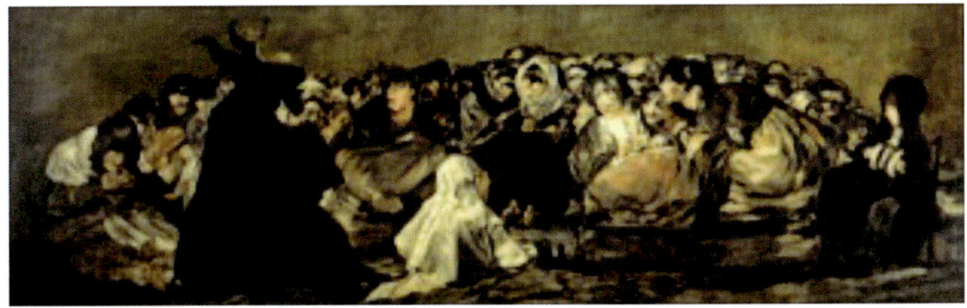

Witches' Sabbath, 1819-1823

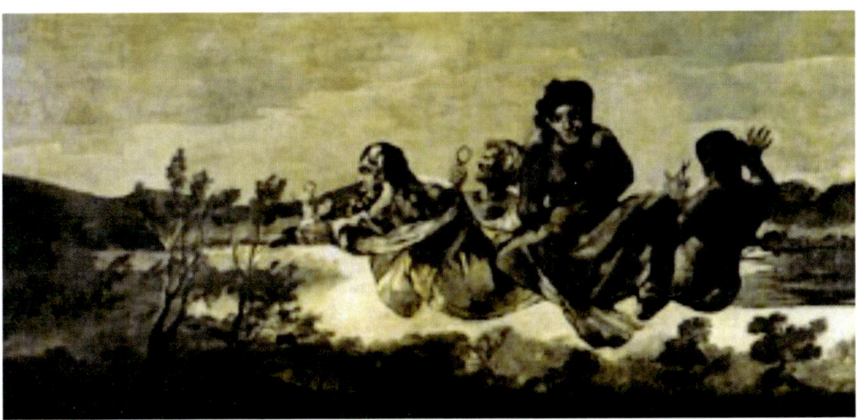

The Black Paintings, an extract from Wikipedia. In 1823 Goya ceded the house, along with the murals, to his grandson Mariano Goya, probably to protect the house from possible reprisals after the restoration of absolute monarchy and repression of liberals by supporters of Fernando VII of Spain. The paintings were little known for half a century. Only certain art critics, such as Charles Yriarte, wrote about them The slow process of transferring the murals onto canvas began in 1874. It was carried out under the

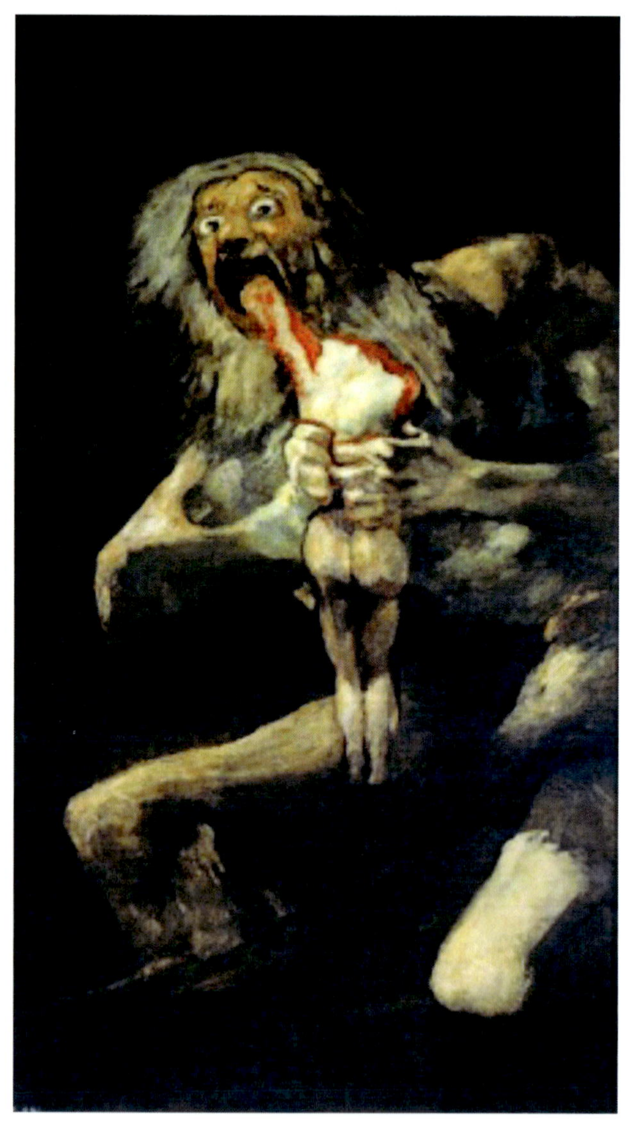

Saturn Devouring His Son, 1819-1823

supervision of Salvador Martínez Cubells at the request of Baron Émile d'Erlanger, a French banker of German origins, who wanted to sell them at the Paris World's Fair in 1878. However, in 1881 the baron donated the paintings to the Spanish state and they are now on display at the Museo del Prado.

Bio-data with acknowledgments
Source: biography.com

The Artist
The son of a gilder, Goya spent some of his youth in Saragossa. There he began studying painting around the age of fourteen. He was a student of José Luzán Martínez. At first, Goya learned by imitation. He copied the works of great masters, finding inspiration in the works of such artists as Diego Rodríguez de Silva y Velázquez and Rembrandt van Rijn.

Later, Goya moved to Madrid, where he went to work with brothers Francisco and Ramón Bayeu y Subías in their studio. He sought to further his art education in 1770 or 1771 by traveling to Italy. In Rome, Goya studied the classic works there. He submitted a painting to a competition held by the Academy of Fine Arts at Parma. While the judges liked his work, he failed to win the top prize.

Goya and The Spanish Court
Through the German artist Anton Raphael Mengs, Goya started to create works for Spain's royal family. He first painted tapestry cartoons, which were artworks that served as models for woven tapestries, for a factory in Madrid. These works featured scenes from everyday life, such as "The Parasol" (1777) and "The Pottery Vendor" (1779). In 1779, Goya won an appointment as a painter to the royal court. He continued to rise in status, receiving admission into the Royal Academy of San Fernando the following year. Goya began to establish a reputation as a portrait artist, winning commissions from many in royal circles. Works, such as

"The Duke and Duchess of Osuna and their Children" (1787-1788), illustrate Goya's eye for detail. He skillfully captured the tiniest elements of their faces and clothes.

Illness

In 1792, Goya became completely deaf after suffering from an unknown malady. He started to work on non-commissioned paintings during his recovery, including portraits of women from all walks of life. His style changed somewhat as well. Continuing to thrive professionally, Goya was named the director of the Royal Academy in 1795. He may have been part of the royal establishment, but he did not ignore the plight of the Spanish people in his work. Turning to etchings, Goya created a series of images called "Los Caprichos" in 1799, which has been viewed his commentary on political and social events. The 80 prints explored the corruption, greed, and repression that was rampant in the country. Even in his official work, Goya is thought to have cast a critical eye on his subjects. He painted the family of King Charles IV around 1800, which remains one of his most famous works. Some critics have commented that this portrait seemed to be more a caricature than a realist portrait.

Goya also used his art record moments of the country's history. In 1808, France, led by Napoleon Bonaparte, invaded Spain. Napoleon installed his brother Joseph as the country's new leader. While he remained a court painter under Napoleon, Goya created a series of etchings depicting the horrors of war. After Spanish royalty regained the throne in 1814, he then painted "The Third of May," which showed to the true human costs of war. The work depicted the uprising in Madrid against French forces.

Final Years

With Ferdinand VII now in power, Goya kept his position in the Spanish court despite having worked for Joseph Bonaparte. Ferdinand reportedly once told Goya that "You deserve to be garroted, but you are a great artist so we forgive you." Others in Spain were not so lucky as the king sought to crackdown on liberals who sought to make the country a constitutional state. Despite the personal risks, Goya expressed his dissatisfaction with the Ferdinand's rule in a series of etchings called "Los disparates." These works featured a carnival theme and explored folly, lust, old age, suffering and death among other issues. With his grotesque imagery, Goya seemed to illustrate the absurdity of the times. The political climate subsequently became so tense that Goya willingly went into exile in 1824. Despite his poor health, Goya thought he might be safer outside of Spain. Goya moved to Bordeaux, France, where he spent the remainder of his life. During this time, he continued to paint. Some of his later works included portraits of friends also living in exile. Goya died on April 16, 1828, in Bordeaux, France.

Personal Life

Goya married Josefa Bayeu y Subías, the sister of his art teachers Francisco and Ramón Bayeu y Subías. The couple had one child who lived to be an adult, their son Xavier.

Cite This Page

APA Style

Francisco de Goya. (2015). The Biography.com website. Retrieved 10:46, Mar 29, 2015, from http://www.biography.com/people/francisco-de-goya-9317129.

Harvard Style

Francisco de Goya. [Internet]. 2015. The Biography.com website. Available from: http://www.biography.com/people/francisco-de-goya-9317129 [Accessed 29 Mar 2015].

MLA Style

"Francisco de Goya." Bio. A&E Television Networks, 2015. Web. 29 Mar. 2015.

The Author Edward Lucie-Smith is an art critic and art historian, also a poet and photographer. He is generally regarded as the most prolific and widely published writer on contemporary art. Some of his books are used as standard texts throughout the world.

LONDON TERMINAL

FRIEZE ART FAIR 2013

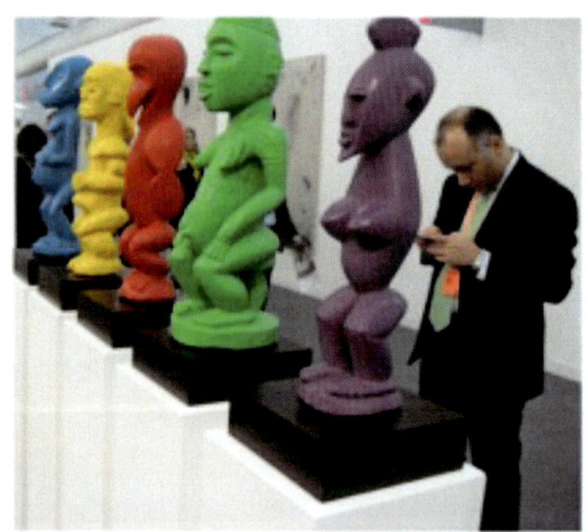

EDWARD LUCIE-SMITH

Cv/Visual Art Research Series 187

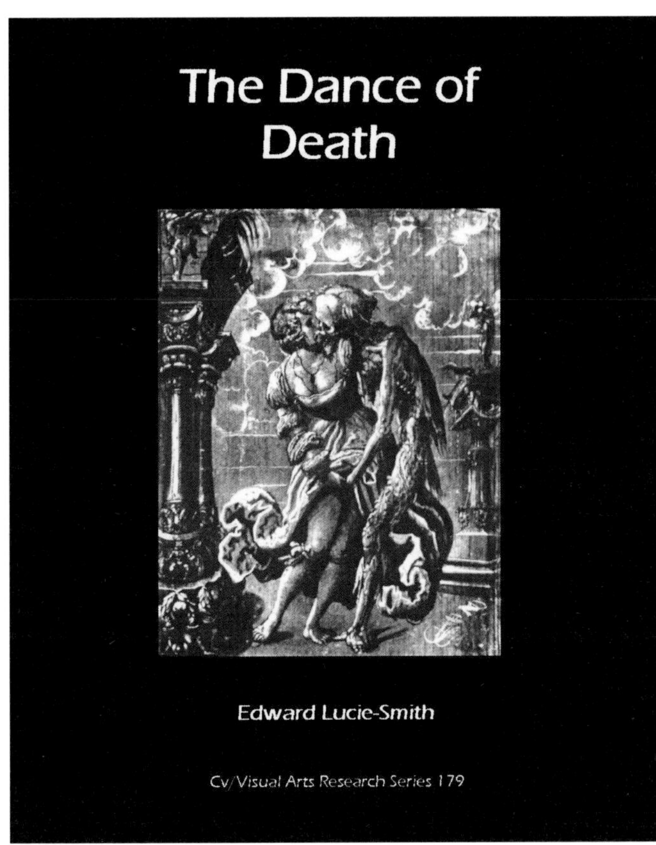
The Dance of
Death
Edward Lucie-Smith
Cv/Visual Arts Research Series 179

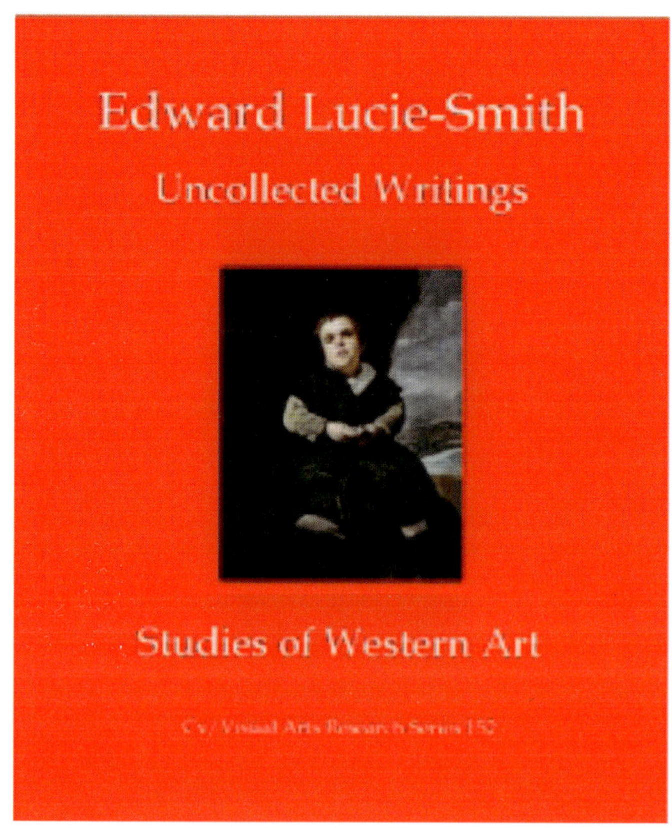
Edward Lucie-Smith
Uncollected Writings
Studies of Western Art

Cv/Visual Arts Research Archive

THE DECLINE AND FALL OF THE AVANT-GARDE

ESSAYS ON CONTEMPORARY ART BY EDWARD LUCIE-SMITH

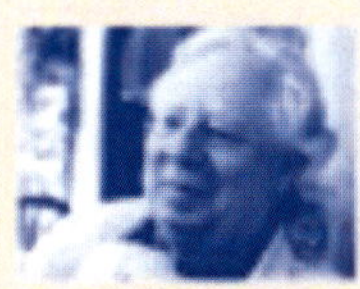

Cv/Visual Arts Research Series 161-175

Art . Travel . Histories

Cv/Visual Arts Research

tracksdirectory.ision.co.uk